T0267662

Many Poems

Roberta Iannamico

Translated by Alexis Almeida

The Song Cave

The Song Cave
www.the-song-cave.com
© Roberta Iannamico, 2024

Design and layout by Janet Evans-Scanlon

ISBN: 979-8-9878288-8-5
Library of Congress Cataloguing-in-Publication Data has been applied for.

FIRST PRINTING

Contents

LIKE GEPPETTO

In the belly of the whale
lighting a candle to write
the ribs are
a colorless rainbow
a temple
where I can hear
my own voice
far from the ocean
dancing alone

NIGHT

Quiet night
barely a breeze
humid and fresh
it's clear
the moon is shining
like a midnight sun
and the night animals
sing
crickets toads dogs
black trees
the gristly flapping
of a bat's wing
you can briefly hear
the sound of a bird
(it's dreaming)
a shooting star
flies over my house

ROCKS

There used to be rocks
big and wild
along the path
to the mountain
the rocks are so hard
they don't need skin
although water leaves its mark
a soft skin
and the wind
a kind of chicken skin
in the shade they're cold
and they're warm in the sun
there's one the shape of a shoe
or a dog's head
and another the shape of a frog
which is one of the most common shapes
among the rocks
a tree grew over a rock
it attached itself to her
and took her exact form
the root couldn't enter
like it could the earth
a tree that lived off the rain
or the air
or love for its rock.

CONVERSATION

I didn't see this
but I know it happened:
my mom in the kitchen
moving her hands
over the counter
handling plates pots
spoons vegetables
my brother in the yard
so small that I
had not even been born
in the skylight
a little plastic doll
with tiny red glasses
that my mom made talk
in a made-up voice
—hi little coconut—
they talked
all morning

A SNOW STORY

On a snow day
many things can happen
for example
walking through the snow
in an open field
leaving footprints
and seeing
that from a completely white hill
someone else is coming down
dressed in a beautiful color
regal
you're walking along the same path
from distinct positions
and at a certain point
you'll meet.

TO LIGHT A CIGARETTE

If it's a shared light
suddenly quiet
and afterwards a shyness
like looking at someone in the eye
with a match
burning low
that we quickly extinguish
with the car lighter
a long kiss
passionate
with the water heater's flame
on the tip of your toes
like kissing your tall boyfriend
with a tiny branch
taken from the fire
satisfied
from being part
of the nature
of this nearby heat
asking someone else to light it
playing the queen.

CLOUDS

The scene:
a field
between two mountains
in which you see:
just that
and the sky
a perfect blue
and voluptuous
clouds
well-formed
that make you want to jump
and roll around inside them
but you can't
because they're made of smoke
a body passes through them
now they go in clumps
and hide
behind the mountain
where they get dressed up
fluff their feathers
one appears
as the protagonist
lilting
lyrical
full of herself
behind the others

like a group of young dancers
in love with making the rounds
a gathering of clouds
begin to appear
the wind pushes an enormous one
that from the side enters the scene
it's a love story
lovers approaching each other
ominously
lovingly
they perch themselves
one on top of the next
just like I dreamed
a gathering of clouds approaching each other
at full speed.

HAPPY RETURNS

The arrival home
a certain kindness
awakens in me
I'm coming
from a faraway place
to another place
also far
perhaps the distance
is me
but for now:
I'll turn toward my chores

I WAS ALWAYS A CLOWN

I made clumsiness funny
if I fell on my ass
if ice cream dripped on me
if I crashed my bike into the wall
now for example
I walk like a vagabond
in a creek without water
and I don't care about anything
and I want
to be happy.

DRESSES

I think a dress
is the best kind of garment
for the spirit
and more so if it's light
long
languid
there are dresses
that are spirits
on their own

FELINEZCO

The granddaughter and the niece
dressing Lina
dead
in the bedroom
of her old house
they put on her favorite clothes
and perfumed her
meanwhile
they had to fill out forms
meanwhile
family arrived
and at around the same time
the pizza and the hearse.

LEFT BEHIND

In my sweatpants under my nightgown
the plates on the counter
call out to me
outside, on the only sunny corner
that undulating silence
that says Lorca
the trees with tall hairdos
and the weeds a bit wild

THE WIND IS MY COMPANION

If I'm alone
it always comes
to say things
in my ear
a long thing
the wind tells me
at the beginning of the road
as if I couldn't already hear it
its arrogance
annoys me some
but afterwards
I don't understand why
I'm alone in this giant field
recently planted
with barely green grass
recently born
the wind blows over it
lays it on the earth
and suddenly I feel soft
its voice that angers me
also sings for me
and I let the wind come with me
each time a bit stronger
in its own voice

and I feel walked across
totally given over to it
trees sing and dance
and when it settles
it feels like peace.

THE WIND IS INSUFFERABLE

It insists
I try not to listen
despondent
I hide my bad mood
the wind
isn't satisfied
with a love poem
it wants everything
your heart
in a heart filled with light
many things can also enter
a heart filled with night
and in a wind-filled heart
only wind enters
too much of it
it should learn how to act
or stay asleep

I SLEEP WITH THEM BOTH

I sleep with them both
like a lion
with her cubs
in the dark
my breathing is soft
like a sheet
theirs is strong
and full of light.

HAPPY BIRTHDAY

University notebook
triangular ruler
papermate
instant-ink
I'm overcome
by such riches
all this technology
to write is to graffiti
always
to break-up the blankness of the wall
and its message
draw on the cave stone
put your hands there
yesterday I passed by in an airplane
and I wrote your name in the sky
you didn't see?
it's not true
but it would have been nice
an over-the-top banner
a gift
for your birthday
like a t-shirt that says
the word "love"
today I'm going to dress up
for you
I'm going cook delicious things

for you
and maybe write
some poems
it's raining in this galaxy
we take shelter
in homes.

SOMETHING INVISIBLE

It's cloudy
and suddenly
on the grass
an oval of sun
in the middle of the scene: nobody
something invisible
intangible
dissolves in the air
it comes from the sun
made a hole in the cloud
and escaped
fell asleep on the grass
giving it heat.

CONCERT

To hear the bird songs
they're all singing
because the air is free
some are soloists
others sing duets
each one in its moment
some introduce
the ones that follow
others are
the impassioned public
and the pigeons: hysterics

DISCIPLE

Finally!
Get outside!
Into the sun!
Hello wise one!
Show me the way
Show me, ant
Show me pillbug
Show me wind
and I'll dance and sing to your spirit
and softness
children,
show me

TO WAKE UP

He kisses me
in the morning
I think love
is an animal
a closeness of snouts
he's a dog
and I could be a cat
with a wide face

EVENING

The quiet of the evening
two birds conversing
one above and one below
like old friends
the lower one gets close to me
makes me her business
she's a baker
a chivalrous townsperson
she goes
leaving as she came
she's taking
a trip across the earth

NARCISA

The memory of my mother
Narcisa!
in front of the mirror saying
I love myself!
I adore myself!
and blowing herself kisses
from the tips of her fingers
to each cheek
you're so beautiful Graciela!
(with you the mold was broken)
and always at the end
my face
next to hers
in the mirror.

LITTLE SICK ONE

A pot with water
to the side of the bed
embroidered with my hair
a wet rag
on my forehead
icy and hot
under the blankets.

WINTER

Colored wool
across the table
the fire lit
it's finally winter
short days
austere
the fire is
the heart of this house
mine also gives off heat
I exist
all around it

FLICKER

Last night
I was sleeping
and suddenly opened my eyes
and I saw through the window
some moonlight enter
lighting up
two white dresses.

FIVE DAISIES

Watching a waterglass
from which emerge
five daisies
I wanted to write
a poem like William Carlos Williams
they're white from the front
and purple from the back
stems and leaves
that fill with bubbles
the water ripples
with the five young children
five daisies.

SIGH

Such restlessness
said like that
in a deep
but quiet voice
that's how I want to start a poem
about the wind
blowing on the grass
not about me.

THE DOCTOR

With doctors' glasses
serious
studious
with my books on the table
I like to see myself this way
on a calm day
cloudy
warm
and the precise song
of the birds

THE ERRAND

And I entered your house
with my loud friends
embarrassing
in your shy presence
you were making some alterations
to a uniform
that someone had gifted you
who lives by the ocean
a uniform
so that you could work
you had it on
it was a long, closed dress
like lace
like a woman painted
by Monet
you were going to make it
with short sleeves
which would be helpful
at your job
but what was your job exactly?
to find fish in the ocean?
or stars?
pearls?
I went
at twilight
toward the ocean's edge

I was watching the sun
red with a blue veil
before arriving I found you there
and we went together
keeping each other company
on the way to the warehouse

THE TRIP

To go
to that part of the ocean
you quickly got on the bus
and your child-like happiness
when you saw that the air
inside the coach
was actually
transparent water
light and soft
your body in the water
resting
watching your red shoes
move like fish.

THE THINGS

Always with the things
the clothes
the plates
the hard-boiled eggs
the tap water
the scattered toys
something warm
something cold
something soft
something heavy
things that fit
in the palm of my hand
that's what I have
to make a life.

THE HAIRDO

I thought it was a butterfly
but it was actually
a small blue bat
it came out at night
while I was sleeping
so as not to disturb me
with its flapping wings
I trapped it
and put it under my pillow
and kept sleeping
when I got up
Flor, who had been dressing me said
don't be scared
but there's a little blue bat
in your hair
it was what I feared
what I most wanted to avoid
but there it was
gripping my hair
like a glowing clip

QUASIMODO

When the sky and the earth
come together
the world gets larger
to feel
like a lamb shaking
like a hot heart beating
in the middle of everything

WINTER

Today I'm tending the fire
a task I complain about
but that I also love
I feed it
I learn to give it more and more
of what it needs to stay alive

SIESTA

A forest of dried poplars
between two mountains
impressionist poplars
the sun on a winter afternoon
light passing between skinny trunks
the telegraphed trunks
trunks with braille
trunks with writing
and below
a bit of grass
fresh green
some warmed by light yellow
from the sun
a golden shade
from a transparent gold
I put myself
at the foot of the tree
its root was my pillow
you could see the sky
between two mountains.

ECLIPSE

A beautiful sky
came with me to Tornquist
like every Monday sunset
a beautiful sky
and the sun
sometimes I look at it
for a second in the face
in a rapture
shameless and seductive
sometimes it's there
behind the clouds
discrete
which allows me
to forget about it
and quietly watch
the beauty of this sky
white blue pink
moving
like the sea in slow motion
it was the day before yesterday
the moon eclipse
something sad
tragic
menstrual
Julia hurting
help she used to say

mama
mama
the passion
and the moon
making clear
its lack of light
almost dead
humiliated
but it was just a moment
like everything
a time
and its brightness returned
the creatures danced
under the silver light.

THE BED

If it's a big bed
a mother
maybe humble
or aristocratic
if it's messy
everything is allowed
everyone invited
clean sheets recently made
it's an envelope
I'm the letter
I close my eyes
and I'm gone

ROUND

Some trees had grown in a round
forming a circle
with their branches reaching up
like arms
like hands
dark brown trunks
with green shoots
under the sky
in the middle of the field.

THE GIANT

There was a reclined woman
facing up
in the middle of a field
a naked woman
the size of a mountain range
from the road you could see her
under the morning sun
she had long hair
extended
over the grass
I imagine her at night
under the stars

CADENCE

A type of music
that makes clocks
and hearts
jolt
in long sighs
breaths

CURTAIN

I look through the little square
of my dirty window
the birds eat
the crumbs I just swept up
I don't know if the one singing
is Antonia or a pigeon
in the distance dogs bark
every kind
there's no wind today
you could go out
and dance on the street
like a theater of puppets.

FRIDAY

On Fridays you might feel beautiful
maybe because of Venus
I've always loved Fridays
in the morning it's already Friday
with its sensual beauty
in the afternoon turning blue
with a certain feeling
of magic lurking
with lace
you like listening to music
and maybe dancing
a feminine beauty
takes on all the visual and non-visual
forms
of the world
Friday night
is more intense
and it's a paradise
of stars
that like to go out on Fridays
and they burn
even brighter

HAPPY BIRTHDAY TO YOU

Happy
birthday
it's all kids
and balloons that get
their freedom
colorful circles crossing the sky
full of air
many colors
they leave the party
to be part
of the celebration

RAIN

Today it's raining lightly
without pause
a winter day in the middle of summer
a winter rain
with that memory
with that resigned calm
inside the house
lives are pulsating
everyone that lives here
the house pulsates
warm inside
wet outside
like a seed
about to grow

NIGHT

Nuit nuit nuit
begins to light up
with the fireflies
covering the air
it seems like magic
the crickets turn on
the barking turns on
the radio turns on
badly tuned
far away
the blue of the sky
begins to darken
the wind turns on

TEARS

Welcome tears
finally
something comes out of me
that is something of what I am
water
salt
it's a spring
water that hydrates the soul
water that calms me
that pours through the eyes
and our windows
through the nose
the double front door
they're rinsing inside the house
it's shining

GIANT BIRD

There's a giant bird
in the sky
above my house
it looks like a pterodactyl
pure white
like it was made of clouds
so big
it takes up the whole sky
its long wings
are curved at the tips
here below there's wind
and it hardly moves
barely goes anywhere
against the wind
without moving its wings
that's how strong it is
how high

THE YELLOW ROSE

I cut one yellow rose
beautiful and perfect
and I make a little time
because this deserves a poem
you
the first yellow rose
to ever live in my house
people say they're disdainful
or contemptuous
which I don't think are the same
but they say so many things
made of words
made of letters
which don't compare at all
to your softness
or your smell
or your shape
I neglected you
for those stupid claims
I despised you
because of their gossip
I put you in one of my grandmother's vases
and you glowed
in your realness
the girls brought you

to the blue table
the sky you lit up
for them and their chores
gods
making planets.

SAN JUAN

The water from the creek
was magic
I know from its low sound
we wash our faces
from afar
a dog runs up
to stay forever
a clear dog
comes with us
along the walk
one of us discovers
an egg in the grass
fallen from the nest
we shake it
close to the sound
the egg goes tic toc
and opens
was it a bird?
or a dragon?
it was born
like any god is born
we passed it from hand to hand
to feel its heart
ay its heart
like a silent drum.

THREE

The middle one
threw itself to the ground
and made up
a nap for itself
clouds passed by
big and slow
the smallest one
like a bird
let out its voice
the   biggest   one
was me

TO GO OUT AT NIGHT

To go out at night
is to wander
through the street
which is other
ready to be stepped on
ready for people
who go out at night
human encounters
music
laughter and misery
and all of your life
like a wind that runs next to you
little streetlamps
that pass quickly
by your side
a tired freedom
with something exhausted
and something happy

IF SOMEONE TAKES YOU BY THE HAND

If someone takes you by the hand
you realize
that hands have hearts
two hands together
understand each other
more than all the people
more than all the beings
they are together
completely
if someone takes you by the hand
only the hand is alive
and the rest of the body
is passed out
your mind is sleeping
and you go
like a kite
to wherever
most surprises you

ANOTHER WINTER ONE

In winter
everything condenses
into one big thought
the trees the houses
and the people inside
are boiled into everything
the central fire
like in a secret box
life always beating
outside the slow beauty
silent and quiet

TO THE KITCHEN,
WHICH IS YOUR PALACE!

What a beautiful hat
that keeps the head warm
so your ideas
don't escape you
so the embroidery
doesn't fly off
a color so romantic
that my thoughts
feels inspired
but ah! the time has come
to go make food
and the castle falls apart
and the dress changes into a smock
and some sweet matés
the crystal glass
and all of nature
at this humble altar

UNTITLED

We leave the window open
so the sound of the ocean
can come in
the ocean's air
and its rumble
sang us
its sad song
while we were sleeping
it entered through our pores
and our snail-like
ears

THE END OF THE PARTY

The end of the party
has left me
badly injured
with a blow
a bite
in the face
and I was spinning
in my doll dress
to a wild force
no one was stopping it
then the day came
and I got sick

A MEMORY

I remember
I was very young
maybe a teenager
and I was in love
I know because I remember it
that day I felt
closer to the world
we were going to paint something
on a wall
I put on my brother's
long shirt
and stood in line
and took the bus
or maybe I went by foot
but there was too much light
spring-like
and my cheeks
were red
and I don't remember much else
just that shirt
and the sun
and something like freedom
or love.

Acknowledgments

Grateful acknowledgements to the editors of *mercury firs*, *FENCE*, and *Harp & Alter*, where several of these translations have appeared. Thank you to Roberta for your poems, and thank you to Ben and Alan for The Song Cave.

OTHER TITLES FROM THE SONG CAVE: